WHAT OTHERS ARE SAYING ...

"Weinstein approaches nutrition and exercise with military precision."
— The Miami Herald

"Inspirational and energetic"
— Green Bay Packers

"Superb and engaging"
— Baptist Health

WHERE COLONEL WEINSTEIN HAS BEEN FEATURED:

Baptist Health Hospitals

Fitness Magazine

The History Channel

Fox Sports Net

The Washington Times

The Las Vegas Tribune

Eurosport, the largest European satellite and cable network

Gold Coast Magazine

Many Others

Develop a long-term perspective of your life. Everything you say, do and think on a daily basis will impact your health, finances and relationships.

- Lt. Col. Bob Weinstein, USAR-Ret.

Quotes

to live by

Lt. Col. Bob Weinstein, USAR-Ret.

Take back control of your health, finances, relationships and spiritual life.

The Health Colonel Series™
www.TheHealthColonel.com

Quotes to live by - Take back control of your health, finances, relationships and spiritual life.
By: Lt. Col. Bob Weinstein, USAR-Ret.
(Lt. Col. Joseph R. Weinstein, USAR-Ret.)
www.TheHealthColonel.com
757 SE 17th Street, #267
Fort Lauderdale, Florida 33316
954-636-5351

Copyright © 2010 Lt. Col. Joseph R. Weinstein, USAR-Ret.
All Rights Reserved.
ISBN: 0984178325
EAN-13: 9780984178322
Published by: The Health Colonel

The Health Colonel Series™

Library of Congress Control Number: 2009909980

This book and parts thereof may not be reproduced in any form, stored in a retrieval system or transmitted in any form by any means (electronic, mechanical, photocopy, recording or otherwise) without prior written permission of the author, except as provided by United States of America copyright law.

Unless otherwise indicated, all scripture quotations are taken from the Holy Bible, New Living Translation, copyright © 1996. Used by permission of Tyndale House Publishers, Inc., Wheaton, Illinois 60189. All rights reserved.

ISBN 978-0-9841783-2-2

Printed in the United States of America

Quotes
to live by

Lt. Col. Bob Weinstein, USAR-Ret.

Take back control of your health, finances, relationships and spiritual life.

The Health Colonel Series™
www.TheHealthColonel.com

Always state your goals in the present tense as if they have already been achieved. Never back off with "maybe" or "I'll try" or "Let's see what happens." Put on your commander's hat and take charge of your goals and your life.

- Lt. Col. Bob Weinstein, USAR-Ret.

CONTENTS

Quotes to live by

Foreword 4

Chapter I - Values, Character and Ethics 7

Chapter II - Goals 25

Chapter III - Health and Fitness 33

Chapter IV - Love, Humility and Spiritual 47

Index 67

About the Author 82

Workshops and Seminars 84

Products 86

Quick Order Form 89

Foreword

Several years ago I attended a general contractor's meeting with all the contractors and subcontractors for a major commercial construction project. Timelines, tasks and subtasks were discussed. Deliverables were discussed. The project was one immense team effort to complete the project on time. One of the supervisors responsible for sealing and coating the floors asked the general contractor, "What's the standard to apply?" My thought was that of course a high standard should apply. But there was more to his question. The supervisor was really asking what the expectations were and he was looking for concrete answers. This is exactly how you should approach your reading of these quotes. Set expectations to be the best you can be.

Most of the quotes in this book are from me. Those that are not are designated as such. There are important questions you need to ask yourself as you read and reflect and apply these quotes to your life. Some of these questions may be:

- Are you asking of yourself concrete questions about improving your finances, your marriage, your health, your relationships and your spiritual life?
- What is the standard you apply when leading your life?
- What expectations of yourself do you have?
- Are you taking responsibility for your life decisions?
- Are you making corrections along the way?
- When you fail or fall behind, do you get right back up, dust yourself off and continue with your worthy life goals?
- Do you ask tough life questions?
- Do you have the courage to change for the better if it is a struggle to do so?

- Are you willing to strive for true happiness and fulfillment?
- Can you apply one quote a day to your life and something to improve upon?

These quotes are a reflection of my personal journey through life. My wish is that they support, inspire and encourage you in yours.

Lt. Col. Bob Weinstein, USAR-Ret.
Professional Speaker, Author and Fitness Boot Camp Instructor
www.TheHealthColonel.com

Chapter 1

Values, Character and Ethics

When you are making decisions at work or home, are you guided by mostly what is comfortable or what is right?

Do we really need conspiratorial help from the government to sabotage our lives? Are we not the greatest saboteurs of our own lives?

It is honorable to be a warrior and soldier. As with being a good soldier there are core values and character qualities that make up being a good citizen.

Be the one whom others can depend upon. Be there for your friends, family, employer, government or other organization you belong to.

Always be respectful when dealing with others. No exceptions.

Practice and live by the Golden Rule. Do unto others as you would have them do unto you. This, of course, requires you to be kind to yourself as well.

If you're wrong, say so. It's honorable. If you may be wrong, say so. It's honorable. If someone makes a mistake or has behaved towards you in a less than honorable manner, be honorable and respectful.

Character values, like muscles, need to be worked on a regular basis to get and stay strong. "Use it or lose it" applies to character values as well.

Don't ever let anyone tell you or convince you that character is not important or that character cannot be changed. Improve your character and you will improve your success in the areas of health, fitness, finances and relationships.

The end does not justify the means. Motive always matters.

The more you do what is right in the course of your life, the more motivated and energize you become to continue on this path and to take it to the next level.

Discouraging and disempowering talk and self-talk will drain you of the positive emotions you need to accomplish life's many tasks, excel at work and nurture relationships.

Take charge and take responsibility for your life with a winning attitude. If the cause is worthy, never, ever give up.

A prudent person foresees the danger ahead and takes precautions; the simpleton goes blindly on and suffers the consequences. - *Proverbs 22:3, Holy Bible, New Living Testament*

Don't be selfish; don't live to make a good impression on others. Be humble, thinking of others as better than yourself. Don't think only about your own affairs, but be interested in others, too, and what they are doing. *Source: Philippians, Chapter 2, vs. 3 – 4, Holy Bible, New Living Translation*

Love those who are your enemy or are against you in any way or who don't share your view of the world, and you are taking the Golden Rule to its highest level. You will be blessed. Such deeds do not go unnoticed by the Creator.

If your enemies are hungry, give them food to eat. If they are thirsty, give them water to drink. - *Source: Proverbs 25: 21-22, Holy Bible, New Living Translation*

The opposite of love is hate and hate kills. It "kills" the person with hate in his or her heart. It kills others and is the catalyst for killing both in connection with a faith and when it is secular based.

Truth is unshakable and independent of how we perceive it, ignore it, reject it or accept it.

Every word of praise and kindness to others actually programs yourself in a very positive way, uplifting your spirit and empowering you to:

- perform better
- have better relationships
- deepen your understanding of what is really important
- raise your self-esteem
- become a magnet for positive change
- attract others to want what you have

The laws of giving and forgiving are more important than the law of attraction.

CHAPTER ONE: VALUES, CHARACTER AND ETHICS

What will be your legacy? Live your life in such a way that you will be remembered as someone who put others first.

Why is there so little mention of the importance of seeking and applying wisdom? It is a mystery.

Adversity is the ultimate test of character.

Testing attitude and character is like a juicer. Once you put the squeeze on, whatever is inside will come out. What is inside of you?

In the face of adversity is when we have the greatest opportunity to "see" ourselves and find our true purpose in life (= our calling). Our calling will give us such deep fulfillment that no amount of money in the world could entice us to abandon it.

Adversity causes our ego to fall by the wayside and make us humble and ready to self-evaluate (= take inventory).

Although personal development is considered a high priority because of its impact on lives of others, it receives, as a rule, a very small amount of our attention.

Personal development is not our purpose and calling. It is an imperative tool to improve oneself. Increased time for personal development would save marriages, prevent wars and cause nations to interact more peacefully. It would also result in a significant reduction of crime.

Those things that are called natural laws are as founded and valid as the laws of physics. They are written on the hearts of every man and woman of every race and creed.

Do we look everyone in the eyes when we greet and interact with them, or only those who are "worthy"? This is the ultimate daily test of how we "see" others and ourselves.

Receive special blessings by giving on a daily basis. It is the equivalent of gathering riches. Giving means not just material things. It starts with a sincere smile with sincere caring for every person you meet.

Similar to the audio quality adjustments on a stereo or computer it is the same way that we maintain the balance of the various values of life. The state of mind of the one who makes the adjustments will determine the level of quality of the tone.

Wisdom will multiply your days and add years to your life. If you become wise, you will be the one to benefit. If you scorn wisdom, you will be the one to suffer. - *Prov. 9:11-12*

Keep things in perspective. We are all here on this earth for a short time.

Whatever measure you use in giving - large or small - it will be used to measure what is given back to you. If you give, you will receive. - *Luke 6:38, Holy Bible, New Living Translation*

Wherever your treasure is, there your heart and thoughts will also be. - *Luke 12:34, Holy Bible, New Living Translation*

How important is receiving a phone call? Very, especially for someone who is alone and lonely. Make that call today.

Are you connected with what you know to be right?

Why do we sometimes tell our children to do things that contradict what we do in our own lives? Why?

Why do we tell a child to always tell the truth when we are many times seeking the "best" excuse or story which is fabricated?

Why do we have such great difficulty keeping a secret or something confidential in us by someone who trusted us to do so?

If you are focusing on your needs, you will not be in a position to recognize the needs of others. Of course your needs are important. You will be pleasantly surprised at the level of personal fulfillment and joy (= your needs) by focusing on the needs of others. Be prepared for a tremendous support group of people caring for one and other who now understand and grasp the philosophy of givers gain.

How we deal with our own flaws and inadequacies will determine how others react to what we say.

Slaves do what others want; servants do what others need.

Humility is being authentic and without pretense or arrogance.

Mercy triumphs over prejudice.

Some people equate being honest with making negative statements.

When you feel positive about a situation, your life seems to draw even greater good to that circumstance. The same power of a positive attitude exists in giving thanks in advance through affirmative prayer.

Be clear about who you are. If you are not sure, you will crumble under pressure. It is in crisis that your true character surfaces.

Be careful about how you spend your money.

We all have a deficit or debt in praising others as we go through life. Seek out every opportunity to praise others.

Perhaps

Perhaps you are negative with yourself.
Perhaps you complain too much.
Perhaps you don't praise others enough.
Perhaps you are not expressing gratitude enough.
Perhaps you are not learning enough.
Perhaps you need to become more teachable.

Negativity is like a skunk spraying you-know-what in all directions. It is not a way to attract people or solutions or success or friends.

Feed your body!
Feed your mind!
Feed your soul!

The key question to ask yourself in the course of the day to check on your own behavior and thoughts: "Is that the person I want to be?"

When you give a gift or a helping hand, whether money or things, never ever hold it against the receiver or mention it in a negative way regardless of the behavior of the recipient after receiving the gift. Whenever you talk about the gift or the help you provided, it should only be for positive reasons to reaffirm reasons you gave the gift in the first place.

Never miss an opportunity to say, do or think the right thing, even under fire, assault and insult.

Stop leading your life like one of those Chinese firecrackers. When you light the fuse, it goes "bang, bang, bang," and it's all over.

Wisdom and insight are especially needed when dealing with difficult people. Be firm, yet kind and sensitive to their "plight." Maintain their self-esteem while addressing the issue.

It is the struggle that offers up the opportunity to strengthen character. Character is not some pie-in-the-sky ideal. Good character is made up of timeless values that benefit oneself and mutually benefit others.

At all times be willing to express what is honorable and true to yourself and your God.

Your practiced standards and expectations will determine the quality of your life. Set and practice high standards to lead a high quality life.

Having money problems? Check to make sure that you treat money with respect. If you don't respect money, it will leave you. If you respect it by using it wisely, it will stay with you and multiply.

Tell all who are in your life why you are thankful for them.

When is the best time to apply wisdom? Every single time, without exception.

The absence of wisdom in decision making is the primary reason for taking a wrong path in life.

Be a constant learner. Maintain a childlike curiosity about life and people with a constant focus on improving your character and behavior.

Like the waves of the ocean we influence all people we come in contact with. That is how we change the world. That is how we can turn bad behavior into good behavior.

Tell someone close to you how much you need them. Tell them why you need them.

If you beat up on yourself in a nonproductive, negative way, you will eventually do the same with others.

Take nothing and no one for granted.

Never be indifferent towards life and the well being of others.

We all have a debt I call the praise account. This is one debt that is never completely paid. Seek out and express specific praise everywhere you go.

Get addicted to seeking out and doing the right thing.

When being critical with yourself, never demean yourself or diminish your self-worth. Remain upbeat and positive. You are your very own best friend. Treat yourself that way.

We have all heard the military term command and control. That is what we need to do with our lives. Take command and control of your life.

It is not a lie when I say I'm feeling great. It is sometimes simply the forced truth.

Never say about someone, "That's the way he or she is." Say instead, "That's what's inside right now."

When discussing a controversial political or philosophical issue, focus on the issue and not on attacking the person. Attacking the person is poison for your own soul and psyche and questions the dignity of the other person.

The Translator

- Live hard, die young.
    Translation: Life is so painful that I need a heavy dose of distraction. Doesn't really matter if it kills me early but "die young" just empowers me to do things that are harmful.

- I'm too old to exercise.
    Translation: It's too much for me. I'm afraid I might hurt something. It's too strenuous.

- I don't have the time.
> Translation: I'm not willing to take a close look at my priorities and make the time for what is important. I'm not willing to give up anything in my present lifestyle even if it means that I'll live healthier and happier.

There are three ways to increase happiness. Count your blessings. Think carefully about how you spend your time after work and cultivate friendships.

Have you ever …
> been overwhelmed by the spirit of God?
> opened your heart to true joy?
> helped someone in need?
> encouraged a homeless person?
> said a kind word to a troubled youth?

In difficult financial times our charitable organizations also suffer. You can always give something, even if it's less. Never stop giving to help others.

Avoid a victim mentality in hard times. That will make you prey to the circumstances. And we all know what happens to prey. The predator is not far behind.

If you say you have forgiven someone but you are not willing to talk to them, you have not forgiven and you will suffer the consequences.

Just start talking

Talk change.
Talk improvement.
Talk aspirations.
Talk possibilities.
Talk overcoming.

Just start talking.
Talk about the plan.
Talk about the key questions in life.
Then start moving.

Give yourself permission to be you, then follow-through.

Develop a bounce back attitude. When stuff happens, get back up and keep moving in the right direction. Never let the circumstances have the last word.

If you don't feel like doing what you've recognized to be the right thing to do, pretend you like it and you eventually will.

Think

Think basics.
Think simplicity.
Think specifics.
Think action.
Think goals.
Think brevity.
Think time-lines.

Make complete and utter peace with your past.

What is your self-concept? How do you see yourself?

Some people spend their lives kicking themselves in the butt for some not-so-good things they've done, then turn around and kick themselves in the butt for kicking themselves in the butt.

It is not what we think that reveals what we do; it is what we do that reveals what we think.

Some are so locked into how they see the world that they are oblivious to opportunities to become better people.

If you want progress in any area of your life, you must leave your comfort zone.

Never say you don't need anyone's help in life. Someone is helping you every day, whether it's garbage collection, mail delivery, food, water, AC or heat.

Nine ways of thinking that could lead to your demise:

1. Adopt a pill popping mentality.
2. Adopt a Can't-do-anything-to-change-it mentality.
3. Adopt a closed mind.
4. Fail to ask, "Am I doing all that's reasonably possible?"
5. Adopt a disregard cause-and-effect mentality.
6. Adopt a philosophy of sedentary lifestyle.
7. Adopt a disregard-what-is-most-important mentality.
8. Eat predominantly refined foods.
9. Think that BMI stands for Big Mac Injection.

Know where you're at on any issue or problem or task. Be at peace with the recognition that you don't understand some things or people. Understand that you don't understand.

When asked your name always state it with confidence just like James Bond. I'll bet you know his answer and it is "Bond, James Bond."

Life is dynamic, it's not static. Inner peace does not mean the dynamics of life are eliminated.

Inner peace is not to be confused with indifference.

Self-worth determines how we feel about others.

Avoid toxic mental waste. That is anything your mind takes in that is not beneficial to you or others.

If you really want to find out what your attitude towards yourself, your fellow man and woman and the Creator should be, read the Sermon on the Mount and test yourself. *Sermon on the Mount, Holy Bible, Book of Matthew, Chapter 6*

We always return to whatever our predominant thoughts are. Make sure yours are honorable and beneficial. If not, work on them and make some changes about what you are exposed to in life and, if need be, change the level of influence of your friends and acquaintances.

Be careful about where your wisdom comes from because it may not be wisdom at all.

Always be the better person in the treatment of others. Put on that mental bullet-proof vest so that when the verbal attacks or hurtful words or behavior come in your direction, you're ready to respond in an honorable manner.

Be like a heat-seeking missile when it comes to finding the good in every situation and person. Zero right in on the good.

I can hardly wait to get up in the morning. I don't want to miss anything!

Practice patience, frugality and generosity and you will always have what you need.

Speak up when you have something important to say. Avoid idle, meaningless talk. Be silent when you don't have something beneficial to say.

Never gossip about anyone. It poisons relationships. It poisons the listener and the one gossiping.

Stay away from foul language. It's toxic mental waste.

Chapter II

Goals

Treat your weight loss goal like you have already achieved it.

Exercise must become one of those things that you do regularly without question. Would you think of bathing or brushing your teeth just once?

The more you do what is right in the course of your life, the more motivated and energized you become to continue on this path and to take it to the next level. It becomes fun and it changes your way of thinking for the better.

Doing the right thing begets more of doing the right thing. You actually will have more energy to do so simply by doing so.

In order to go from point A to point B in your life journey, you've got to know where point A is to get to point B.

The real investment is planning and executing your own fitness program as if you were commanding a military operation and your life and the lives of others depended upon it because they do.

Spend most of your time focusing on your worthy goals of tomorrow and not on the problems of yesterday.

Always visualize what you want to accomplish and then live by that visualization and you will make it reality.

Always use deadlines when goal setting and tasking for oneself or others. Once you determine that a task or goal is important enough to be accomplished, don't get distracted by the less important daily activities.

Always think of the long-term, positive impact of a goal or task versus one that is only of short-term benefit.

Don't get side-tracked by the nonessentials.

Sometimes we need to get amnesia about what we think we can't do. Many amazing things have been accomplished simply because of lack of knowledge that it couldn't be done.

Fictitious Danger

This one may be controversial because it operates on the fear mechanism. We should first be inspired to do the right thing. If that doesn't work and the real danger of death and/or disease has not yet arrived, we can scar ourselves into visualizing a long-term threat to such an extent that we really get scared and then immediately make the necessary lifestyle changes to combat the threat of early death and/or disease.

Think, speak and act with awareness. Everything counts (words, deeds and thoughts).

A spirit of discontent is not a solution oriented spirit.

If you are asked, "What are your goals in life, what will be your response?" If any of these are your answers, your life is at a standstill:

- I don't know.
- I'll find out someday.
- What good are goals anyway? I always go back to my old ways.
- I wish someone would tell me what my goals are.
- I just can't stick with it.
- I lose interest.
- I can't seem to find anyone's help.

Key questions to ask:

- Where do you want to be in life?
- How do you need to get there?
- What will it take?
- What obstacles and challenges can be expected along the way?

Do not run your life by following the raisin theory. Those who follow the raisin theory are always trying the pick out the raisins of life by avoiding anything that might require a struggle or effort. Following the raisin theory is a one-way ticket to never succeeding at worthy goals.

If the cause is worthy, always believe in second chances, and third and fourth.

It is the death of a great idea that ultimately causes us to fail. Never give up on a great idea. Give it legs to move with, keep it alive and keep working to make it reality.

Many of us think or say, we will behave differently, when we feel more like doing so. Unfortunately, many times those feelings never come.

Most of the land mines of life have delayed fuses. It may take five, ten or fifteen years for them to go off. We are constantly being informed about these delayed fuse land mines that will hurt our relationships, finances and health.

Become a strategic planner of your life, how you think and how you behave. That will allow you to assess the long-term impact and make adjustments along the way.

Never let hope die when pursuing worthy goals, such as improved character, health, fitness or weight loss.

Always state your goals in the present tense as if they have already been achieved. Never back off with "maybe" or "I'll try" or "Let's see what happens." Put on your commander's hat and take charge of your goals and your life.

No apologies and no excuses! Get up, reassess and take a look at what you can do better. Then move out with confidence and continue to pursue your dreams.

If you're looking to make a positive change in your life, the most important question will be "How bad do you want it?" If you want it bad enough, you will overcome all obstacles.

Turn your dreams into goals and your goals into reality.

Tackle a task today that just can't get done, even though it should.

Impact is more important than intentions. Measure your progress to see if you are achieving your goals or just thinking and talking them to death.

Do not be a mistake avoider. You will not accomplish anything like that.

If you want to predict the future, take a close look at how you live. Everything you do, say and think has a long-term impact and will – to a great extent – determine your future.

Once you make a decision, it must grow legs and move.

Avoid drift once you've started taking the right action. Beware of drift. Drift is what happens when you allow yourself to drift away from the right decision you made.

Put on that take-charge, allow no excuses commander's hat and take back your life.

Focus on what you can do and not what you can't.

Design

Design your time.
Design your day.
Design your relationships.
Design your week.
Design your finances.
Design your business.
Design your free time.
Design your work time.
Design your vacation time
Design your volunteer time.

If we allow a plan to die in our minds, it is dead until we revive it.

On the battlefield, the military goes after the high value enemy targets. Those are the targets that will have the greatest impact. That is how we should approach our goal-setting and implementation as it pertains to our lives.

When working on high value tasks, single-mindedness is the key to getting through the challenging parts.

Find out what's most important in your life, and then do it.

On a scale of one to ten, list your priorities in life. Now take that list and compare it to reality. Your job is now to begin living your priorities.

Develop a long-term perspective of your life. What is a long-term perspective? A long-term perspective is understanding that everything you say, do and think on a daily basis will impact your health, finances and relationships 5, 10, 15 and 20 years from now. Look carefully at how you are living today to make sure that you finish life's race with a winning record of how you lived.

Ten-Percent-Club-Members do the following:

- Practice delayed gratification to stick with their long-term goals.
- Think strategically about the person they want to become and what they want to accomplish in their lifetime.
- Constantly seek and find their purpose in life.
- Never give up.
- Can hardly wait to get up in the morning.

Your level of life expectations set the boundary stones and will determine your health, wealth, happiness, relationships, level of formal and informal education and work ethics.

Dreams are there to become reality. Create that reality by realizing your dreams.

Chapter III

Health and Fitness

Are you looking for medical insurance? Make your premium payments in the form of living a healthy lifestyle void of dependence on a home pharmacy of medications.

We have a health pollution crisis in this country. We are polluting our health by how we live.

Most of our medications are prescribed because of our lifestyles, not because we simply got sick.

There are enemy soldiers on America soil. The names of these soldiers are Heart Disease, Cancer and Stroke. They are killing over 3,000 Americans a day.

I don't associate health with "health" insurance or visiting the doctor. I associate good health with a healthy lifestyle.

Being fit and healthy has nothing to do with eating or exercise and has everything to do with how we think.

We all need a little body fat, so don't go trying to lose body fat till you're skin and bones and can't find anything to pinch.

90% of Americans know that most people are overweight, but only 40% think they are overweight. That's self-deception at work.

CHAPTER THREE: HEALTH AND FITNESS

If you could drink gasoline and the body could process it as food, you would get about 912 MPG while bicycling. A gallon of gas has 31,000 calories.

An important truth to remember for all body types is that regular exercise and healthy eating will make you look better and give you more energy.

Regular exercise is the best health insurance premium, and it doesn't have to cost a thing. In fact, it may even save you a significant amount of money that you would have spent on illnesses, lost workdays and prescription medications.

Develop a philosophy of movement in your life. Incorporate as much exercise and movement into your daily life as reasonably possible. Seek out activities-based things to do with your free time.

Weight-loss <u>without exercise</u> will result in only 3/4's of a pound of fat loss and ¼-pound of muscle loss for every pound lost. Weight-loss <u>with an exercise program</u> will result in 1 and ¼-pounds of fat loss and 1 ¼-pound gain in muscle mass for every pound lost.

All exercise is cumulative. That means every 10, 20, 30, 40 and 60 minute time period for exercise adds up to a cumulative health benefit.

Don't like exercise? Tough! You are hereby ordered to like exercise. Spend every morning and evening in front of the mirror expressing your fondness of exercise. Not liking exercise may kill you before your time or cause you to come down with a disease or incapacitation that will not be fun.

Try a walking meeting at work. Work the body while stimulating creativity. Walking relaxes the body and may promote solution finding for difficult challenges on the agenda.

Do what you say you're going to do. Not following through is a roadblock to permanent weight-loss.

Muscle turns to fat? What a bunch of hogwash! The Wizard of Oz may be able to turn muscle into fat, but that's a fairytale. And by the way, there is no Tooth Fairy!

Fat loss around the waist by doing abs?

You can crunch all day.
You can crunch all night.
You can crunch at bedtime and by the moonlight.
You can crunch it up. You can crunch it down.
There ain't no way you'll lose a pound.

If you don't perform strength training while on a weight-loss program, your body will begin practicing cannibalism. And guess whose muscle mass your body will eat? Your own!

Would you ever hear a race-car driver say, "I'm going to put low-octane fuel in that gas tank." That would kill performance. It's no different with the human body. Put low-octane fuel (= unhealthy food choices) in your body, and your performance and energy level will suffer.

If you are predominantly eating close-to-nature, plant-based, unprocessed foods, you are probably eating healthy. If, on the other hand, you are predominantly eating processed foods and lots of animal products (meat and dairy), you are probably eating unhealthy.

80 % of American executives feel that corporate America has a responsibility to promote wellness. – *Source: Study by the American Management Association, October 2004*

Stronger, healthier and happier Americans are more productive. Inject solid, practiced core and life values into the formula, and the customers and clients will be attracted to your products and services.

According to the Centers for Disease Control, more than 75% of employers' health care costs and productivity losses are related to employee lifestyle choices.

An employee wellness program is just an agenda point, in many cases, for those weekly meetings reserved for a little discussion with a wink and a nod from management and simply moving on to the next agenda point. No action. No impact.

Employers need to understand that whether or not a wellness program to save lives and suffering of those under their supervision is implemented cannot be optional.

Make fitness boot camp a part of your corporate culture and you will build strong teams, increase productivity and improve the lives of your employees.

Without a struggle, there can be no progress.

An object at rest tends to stay at rest and an object in motion tends to stay in motion. - *Sir Isaac Newton*

A baby born in the U.S. in 2004 will live an average of 77.9 years. That life expectancy ranks 42 d in the world, down from 11th twenty years earlier. *Source: Census Bureau and National Center for Health Statistics*

Who is responsible for the health crisis in America? You and I as individuals are personally responsible by the way we lead our lives.

Is there a government conspiracy when it comes to the health crisis in America? Let's get one thing straight. You and I do not need anyone's help in creating a health crisis. You and I are the greatest conspirators of our own lives and lifestyles.

Do not blame any institution or anyone else for your poor choices that lead to disease, illness and poor health.

Teachers are role models and leaders when it come to the eating and exercise habits of our children and how they portray their attitudes about fitness and health in school.
Health insurance does not equate to a healthy lifestyle or good health.

Early in America's pioneer history, schoolteachers were expected to be morally beyond reproach in every detail of their own lives. This reflected how those communities wanted to influence their children's future and the future of the country as a whole.

The poor state of health of Americans is a direct reflection of American culture, a culture of overindulgence, instant gratification and sedentary lifestyle. Change the culture into one of sensible eating and exercise and a new cultural standard is set that will be followed by the masses.

The percentage of children and adolescents who are defined as overweight has nearly tripled since the early 1970's.
- *Centers for Disease Control and Prevention*

Americans and their children are the most over-fed and under-nourished group of people in the world.

Whatever challenges our country faces will be better met if we are healthier in mind and body.

The present health pollution of America is a national security issue because the consequences go much farther into sociological issues, such as increased crime and poor learning ability. An unhealthy America cannot perform or think as well.

Sick and unhealthy Americans are living longer and living with meds. These Americans need to be weaned back to health and off of the meds, where possible.

Lactic acid build-up in muscles will cause pain that will probably not hurt you physically; it will only hurt your feelings.

Employee attitude becomes a reflection of the leader's attitude.

Always be yourself. It's okay to feel comfortable about being you.

Focusing on the negatives will hurt your self-esteem.

Transcend the trend. Beware of all the trends out there offering you quick-fixes to life's challenges. A worthy cause always requires effort and is never quick.

You can't always feel disease prevention and you can't always feel the negative impact at the molecular and cellular level of eating too much refined foods. In the long run you will feel and experience the poor health consequences.

Poor health of Americans is not about obesity. It's not about fat. In many ways, you can neither see nor feel good health inside. Take a look at the research and understand the consequences of an unhealthy lifestyle. Look at the stats. It's very sobering and alarming.

It's not how long we live but how we live that is most important. If we focus on how we live, we will live longer and have a higher quality of life.

Never diet without exercising.

Get amnesia about what you cannot do or achieve.

Don't stop, modify it!

Example: You're jogging and "feel" like you can't continue. Instead of walking, slow your jogging pace, relax your body and relax your breathing.

Calories

- Carbs = 4 cal./gram
- Protein = 4 cal./gram
- Alcohol = 7 cal./gram
- Fat = 9 cal./gram

"There's a War Out Going on Out There!"

Many times during my workouts with clients I get comments and questions. "Where's the war? or "Looks like you're dressed for battle." or "Is there a war going on here?" My response is, "Yes. There is a war going on in America. Unhealthy lifestyles are killing and maiming too many Americans."

Get up and show up!
This is the secret behind keeping an exercise program on track!

Exercise priorities in order of health importance:

1. Cardio
2. Muscle Endurance
3. Muscle Strength
4. Flexibility (= stretching)

Visualize the end results to push the decision to act. Then, focus exclusively on the positive benefits and heightened sense of well-being.

Exercise the mind on concentrating focus on thought. This is to strengthen the "concentration muscle". Helps willpower and discipline.

Treat time like it's your dearest friend.

We are walking around with the most affordable and portable exercise equipment in the world, our bodies.

If you are taking any medication, one of your most important strategies should be to address with your doctor what you can do to get off of medication by making lifestyle changes, such as exercising, eating right and thinking beneficial thoughts. Find ways to get off of drugs safely.

Join the "Department of Push-ups" and you will never have a problem with upper body strength. As a member you are permitted to do push-ups whenever and wherever you like.

You are the lucky winner of 500 push-ups today. You may start using your winnings right away.

Work the mind like a muscle. You don't want to get brain atrophy. That's worse than muscle atrophy.

Substance is more important than form. If you can't use proper form while exercising, you are still taking care of substance (= exercise and movement) as long as you are not injuring yourself.

I'm still looking for a dog that can do push-ups.

Instead of just calories on nutritional food labels, what types of exercise and duration of exercise it takes to burn that food off should be included.

Always stay in touch with your body when exercising. Understand that you do need exertion to make progress. Pace yourself.

If you can't jog, walk. If you can't walk, crawl. If you can't crawl, wiggle.

We were born to do push-ups. It's one of the first moves a baby makes.

Understand that the body does not always perform the same.

It's time for math class. When it comes to exercise, there is only multiplication and addition, no subtraction.

When exercising outdoors, treat your environment like a playground. Look through the eyes of a child on the lookout to enhance the fun factor and you will get a great workout and have a great time doing it.

Nine ways of thinking that could lead to your demise:

Adopt a pill popping mentality.

Adopt a Can't-do-anything-to-change-it mentality.

Adopt a closed mind.

Fail to ask, "Am I doing all that's reasonably possible?"

Adopt a disregard cause-and-effect mentality.

Adopt a philosophy of sedentary lifestyle.

Adopt a disregard-what-is-most-important mentality.

Eat predominantly refined foods.

Think that BMI stands for Big Mac Injection.

LT. COL. BOB WEINSTEIN'S QUOTES TO LIVE BY

Chapter IV

Love, Humility and Spiritual

If you want to be spiritual you need the spiritual "Full Metal Jacket." Be a truth seeker and listen to your heart. The Creator of all that is and ever was will speak to your heart if you humble yourself and are willing to listen.

Spiritual is not about meditating and praying and going to church *unless* the attitude of your heart is in the right place.

Spiritual is about having an open heart and mind to listen to the Creator.

Don't be selfish; don't live to make a good impression on others. Be humble, thinking of others as better than yourself. Don't think only about your own affairs, but be interested in others, too, and what they are doing. *Source: Philippians, Chapter 2, vs. 3 – 4, Holy Bible, New Living Translation*

You must love the Lord with all your heart, all your soul, and all your mind. This is the first and greatest commandment. A second is *equally* important: Love your neighbor as yourself. *Source: Matthew, Chapter 22, v. 36, Holy Bible, New Living Translation*

You have heard that the Law of Moses says, "Love your neighbor and hate your enemy." But I say, love your enemies! Pray for those who persecute you! In that way, you will be acting as true children of your Father in heaven. *Source: Matthew, Chapter 5, v. 43, Holy Bible, New Living Translation*

If your enemies are hungry, give them food to eat. If they are thirsty, give them water to drink. *Source: Proverbs 25: 21-22, Holy Bible, New Living Translation*

Love those who are your enemy or are against you in any way or who don't share your view of the world, and you are taking the Golden Rule to its highest level. You will be blessed. Such deeds do not go unnoticed by the Creator.

The opposite of love is hate and hate kills. It "kills" the person with hate in his or her heart. It kills others and is the catalyst for killing both in connection with a faith and when it is secular based.

There are many religions, some similar, most different. Many will embrace the universal values that have been embedded in our hearts by the Creator. Which one is the right one? All of them? Some of them or just one? Ask God, the Creator of all that is. If you have an open and humble heart and are truly seeking the truth, the Creator will find you.

Will you need a crisis situation of life or death to humble your heart and seek out the Creator and decision maker of all that is? Hopefully not.

The conflict never ends because the real conflict is within, even when leading a spiritual life. To disregard this important truth will make you vulnerable.

After this life on earth is over and you're checking in with the Creator, you might want to be greeted at check in time with "How are you?" and not "Who are you?" If your first greeting from the Creator is "Who are you?" you know you're in trouble.

We're always talking about how important communication is for relationships. This applies to your relationship with the Creator. If you are not communicating with Him on a regular basis, the relationship will suffer.

Truth is unshakable and independent of how we perceive it, ignore it, reject it or accept it.

Watch over your heart. - *Proverbs 4:23*

Fear of the Lord is the beginning of wisdom. Conversely, lack of fear of the Lord will inevitably allow our egos to get involved, cause us to fear others. - *Proverbs 9:10*

The help of God never precludes human action, it always presupposes it.

90 % of all Christians are biblically illiterate.

Every word of praise and kindness to others actually programs yourself in a very positive way, uplifting your spirit and empowering you to:

- perform better.
- have better relationships.
- deepen your understanding of what is really important.
- raise your self-esteem.
- become a magnet for positive change.
- attract others to want what you have.

This life is a test and training grounds. Your mission should be to pass the test. Just remember who the evaluator is, the Creator of all that is and ever was.

The laws of giving and forgiving are more important than the law of attraction.

What will be your legacy? Live your life in such a way that you will be remembered as someone who put others first.

Think about the person you would like to become and not about what you don't like about yourself.

Why is there so little mention of the importance of seeking and applying wisdom? It is a mystery.

Always be yourself. It's okay to feel comfortable about being you.

Focusing on the negatives will hurt your self-esteem.

Who or what is your master? If you are constantly blaming external circumstances for why you can't accomplish something, you are a slave to those circumstances.

What is the best way to find the right answers in life? Find the right questions.

The Creator is more interested in your character than your career.

It's not how long we live but how we live that is most important. If we focus on how we live, we will live longer and have a higher quality of life.

In the face of adversity is when we have the greatest opportunity to "see" ourselves and find our true purpose in life (= our calling). Our calling will give us such deep fulfillment that no amount of money in the world could entice us to abandon it. Adversity causes our ego to fall by the wayside and make us humble and ready to self-evaluate (= take inventory).

Personal development is not our purpose and calling. It is an imperative tool to improve oneself. Increased time for personal development would save marriages, prevent wars and cause nations to interact more peacefully. It would also result in a significant reduction of crime.

Those things that are called natural laws are as founded and valid as the laws of physics. They are written on the hearts of every man and woman of every race and creed.

Do we look everyone in the eyes when we greet and interact with them, or only those who are "worthy"? (Ultimate daily test of how we "see" others and ourselves.)

Receive special blessings by giving on a daily basis. It is the equivalent of gathering riches. Giving means not just material things. It starts with a sincere smile, with sincere caring for every person you meet.

Receive eternal salvation of your soul by recognizing and accepting the power and authority of Jesus Christ.

Religions and personal development courses as well as philosophies all - to various degrees - grasp and practice the natural laws that benefit mankind. They, however, cannot offer eternal salvation of the soul. That is a divine legal act that can only be performed by someone who is empowered to do so.

It is a humbling experience to recognize and acknowledge that you need salvation.

Even if we don't recognize Christ as the savior of our souls, He is - in secular terms - hands down the most important philosopher who has clearly and simply revealed the depth of natural laws of life. He demonstrated and radicalized what practiced true love really means.

If I were given a choice between fulfilling my true purpose in life and doing something else that would result in extreme wealth, I would choose that which is my true purpose. Therein lays true success and happiness. This is one of the areas of life where there should be no compromise.

Horses in a burning barn tend to run back into the fire when rescued because they consider the status quo (= the barn) to be their safe haven. Make sure that your safe haven lifestyle is not a burning barn.

Find out what God likes and then do it.

A positive attitude towards the Creator of all that is and ever was, will allow Him to work in your life.

There are many examples of God changing decisions he had made about mankind and individuals based on their behavior and choices they made. The bible is full of both blessings and curses. There are consequences for everything we do.

Networking means building relationships. The ultimate network is to build a relationship with the Creator of all that is.

The only way to understand the value of a relationship with the Creator is through wisdom.

Wisdom will multiply your days and add years to your life. If you become wise, you will be the one to benefit. If you scorn wisdom, you will be the one to suffer. *Source: Proverbs 9:11-12, Holy Bible, New Living Translation*

Keep things in perspective. We are all here on this earth for a short time.

Whatever measure you use in giving - large or small - it will be used to measure what is given back to you. If you give, you will receive. *Source: Luke, Chapter 6, vs. 38, Holy Bible, New Living Translation*

Is there anything worth more than your soul?

Wherever your treasure is, there your heart and thoughts will also be. *Source: Luke, Chapter 12, vs. 34, Holy Bible, New Living Translation*

Why do we sometimes tell our children to do things that contradict what we do in our own lives? Why?

Why do we tell a child to always tell the truth when we are many times seeking the "best" excuse or story which is fabricated?

Why do we have such great difficulty keeping a secret or something confidential in us by someone who trusted us?

Ten Reasons to Fear God (There are more.)

1. Live a happier life.
2. Fear no one (except God).
3. Save your soul.
4. Live a healthier life.
5. Receive more blessings.
6. Have greater (true) purpose.
7. Have better relationships.
8. Have greater influence.
9. Have greater abundance. Yes, God promised this, too. (material and non-material)
10. Care for all others more, not just those who are "worthy" or who are nice to us. Anyone can do that. That's easy. This is about caring for those who are not nice to us or who "appear" to be less worthy of care. God really likes this.

Wouldn't it be great to meet someone who is uplifting and positive, full of encouragement and compassion regardless of our present life situation, whether rich, poor, homeless, drug problem, obese, beautiful, ugly, fat or skinny? That is Jesus Christ.

CHAPTER FOUR: LOVE, HUMILITY, SPIRITUAL

The meaning of seeking and quest.

- Why climb a mountain?
- What is the motive?
- Is it adventure, curiosity, challenge, seeking purpose for being, improving oneself, creating adversity for self-improvement, deepening spiritual convictions, finding God?

"We're people, just like you. Touch us. Talk to us. Say "Hello" and "Good morning". We made it through the night the same way you did: By the grace of God." *Homeless quote from the Sun-Sentinel, South Florida, 11/05/2004*

We all have a deficit or debt in praising others as we go through the day and life. Seek out every opportunity to praise others.

Perhaps

Perhaps you are negative with yourself.
Perhaps you complain too much.
Perhaps you don't praise others enough.
Perhaps you are not expressing gratitude enough.
Perhaps you are not learning enough.
Perhaps you need to become more teachable.

Ask God and Listen

95% believe in God. Why?
I say ask God and listen.

But I'm not sure of the truth.
I say ask God and listen.

But I'm not worthy.
I say ask God and listen.

But I've hurt too many people.
Ask God and listen.

But I'm afraid of the truth.
Ask God and listen.

I'm afraid of death.
Ask God and listen.

Someone hurt me.
Ask God and listen.

Listen to the souls

Listen to the souls.
They are calling out;
They are sad;
They are scared;
They are lost.

Listen to the souls.
They are wandering;
They are wondering;
They are laughing;
They are crying.

Listen to the souls.
They may act confident;
They may act shy;
They're not really sure how or why.

Listen to the souls.
Listen to the souls.
Listen to the souls.
The many living souls.
Are you listening?
Can you hear their cry for help?
Can you hear their cry for direction?

Feed your body.
Feed your mind.
Feed your soul.

Are you lukewarm about life? When yes, why?

Righteousness means right standing before God. How? Through forgiveness.

Complacency kills. After about 7 years of practicing a certain negative lifestyle, a certain immunity sets in. Seek the help of others and God to cure you of this killer.

When you give a gift or a helping hand, whether money or things, never ever hold it against the receiver or mention it in a negative way regardless of the behavior of the recipient after receiving the gift. Whenever you talk about the gift or help you provided, it should only be for positive reasons to reaffirm reasons you gave the gift in the first place.

Never miss an opportunity to say, do or think the right thing, even under fire, assault and insult.

Sometimes we demean ourselves about our small steps in the right direction, instead of words of encouragement.

CHAPTER FOUR: LOVE, HUMILITY, SPIRITUAL

Hold no grudge against anyone on this Earth. If you do, the Creator of all this is will hold it against you.

Tell all who are in your life why you are thankful for them.

The absence of wisdom in decision making is the primary reason for taking a wrong path in life.

And the spirit cries out ...

Do you care?

A homeless man looking unkempt and dirty walks past you on the sidewalk.
Do you care?

A teenager with tattoos, angry and abused, feeling down and lacking direction.
Do you care?

Someone is dying needlessly of ill health.
Do you care?

Someone is in need of forgiveness.
Do you care?

Some things the Creator of all that is and ever was really likes:

When we ask for his guidance.
When we ask for his forgiveness.
When we forgive others.
When we ask for his strength.
When we ask for his help.
When we help the youth.
When we help someone in need.
When we help the homeless.
When we recognize his authority.
When we are thankful.
When we respect our elders.

Blessings

May you understand that God wants you to succeed in life. May you be blessed with the courage to get back up every time you fall. May you be filled with kindness and compassion for others.

From time to time, personally rededicate all your projects, relationships, clients, finances, food and shelter to the Creator of all that is. He likes that and it reminds you of who is really in charge.

The surest way to be defeated whether on the battlefield or in civilian life is to give up hope.

If you beat up on yourself in a nonproductive, negative way, you will eventually do the same with others.

One person can make a significant difference when focused on helping others.

You must first understand who you are before you can accept the Creator of all that is.

Take nothing and no one for granted.

Never be indifferent towards life and the well being of others.

We all have a debt I call the praise account. This is one debt that is never completely paid. Seek out and express specific praise everywhere you go.

Have you ever …

- been overwhelmed by the spirit of God?
- opened your heart to true joy?
- helped someone in need?
- encouraged a homeless person?
- said a kind word to a troubled youth?

In difficult financial times our charitable organizations also suffer. You can always give something, even if it's less. Never stop giving to help others.

Honor the Lord with your wealth and with the best part of everything your land produces. Then he will fill your barns with grain, and your vats will overflow with the finest wine.
- *Proverbs 3: 9 - 10*

Make complete and utter peace with your past. If you were to pray a daily prayer about your life what would it be? What would it cover?

A person who has a humble and sincere relationship with the Creator is well respected. We feel that he or she is in touch and nurtures his or her relationship with God.

Some are so locked into how they see the world that they are oblivious to opportunities to become better people.

A true and persistent seeker finds answers.

If you really want to find out what your attitude towards yourself, your fellow man and woman and the Creator should be, read the Sermon on the Mount and test yourself. *Sermon on the Mount, Holy Bible, Book of Matthew, Chapter 6*

Be careful about where your wisdom comes from because it may not be wisdom at all.

Truth is unshakable and independent of how we perceive it, ignore it, reject it or accept it.

CHAPTER FOUR: LOVE, HUMILITY, SPIRITUAL

One day that trash collector with a humble heart, full of love and respect for people and the Creator will be put in charge of God's domains.

According to an ancient law, when the farmer harvests grain he should always leave some for the needy and the foreigners. When you harvest your paycheck, do the same. Leave some for those less fortunate than you.

LT. COL. BOB WEINSTEIN'S QUOTES TO LIVE BY

Index

3
31,000 calories 35

9
912 MPG 35

A
Abundance 56
Addition 44
Adversity 11, 52
Afraid 58
Amnesia 27, 41
Ancient law 65
Answers 64
Appreciation 17
Ask God and Listen 58
Aspirations 20
Attitude 14, 20, 23, 48, 54, 64
    exercise 36
Authority 62
Awareness 27

B
Baby 44
Balance 12
Be yourself 40
Behavior 15, 17, 18, 29, 54
Being wrong 8
Bible 9, 10, 12, 23, 48, 49, 54, 64

Big Mac Injection... 45
Biking... 35
Blame.. 38
Blessings... 12, 53, 54, 56, 62
BMI.. 22
Body... 15
Body fat.. 34
Brain... 43
Burning barn... 54

C

Calling.. 52
Calories... 41, 43
Cancer.. 34
Cannibalism.. 36
Can't-do-anything-to-change-it mentality................. 45
Cardio... 42
Career... 52
Caring.. 13, 56
Catalyst for killing.. 49
Cause-and-effect.. 45
Centers for Disease Control... 37
Change... 20, 26
Character... 52
    strengthening.. 16
    test.. 11, 14
Character values.. 8
Charitable organizations... 63
Charity.. 19
Child... 44, 55
Children... 13, 48, 55
    overweight statistics.. 39
Choice.. 54
Christians.. 50
Church... 48

Circumstances	20, 52
Close-to-nature food	37
Closed mind	22, 45
Comfort zone	21
Command and control	18
Commandment	48
Communication	50
Compassion	62
Complacency	60
Complaining	15, 57
Compromise	54
Concentration	42
Confidence	22, 29
Confidentiality	13, 56
Conflict	49
Consequences	9, 19, 54
Conspiracy health	38
Contradiction	55
Controversy	18
Corporate culture	38
Courage	62
Creator	10, 23, 48, 49, 52, 54, 62, 64
Crime	11, 52
Crisis	14, 49
Critical	18
Curiosity	17
Curses	54

D

Danger	27
Deadlines	27
Death	49, 58
Debate	18

Debt	17, 57, 63
Decision	49
Decisions	8, 30
Deficit	57
Demean	18, 60
Demise	45
Department of Push-ups	43
Dependability	8
Dependance on the help of others	21
Design	31
Desire	30
Dieting	41
Difficult people	16
Dignity	18
Discontent	27
Disease prevention	40
Disregard-what-is-most-important mentality	45
Distraction	18
Doctor	43
Dog	43
Doing the right thing	9, 13, 17, 20, 26
Dreams	29, 30, 32
Drugs	43

E

Earth	50, 55
Ego	52
Elders	62
Employee attitude	40
Employee wellness program	37
Empower	10
Empowerment	51
Encouragement	60, 63
Enemies	48
Enemy	10, 49

Enemy soldiers	34
Enthusiasm	23
Environment	44
Eternity	53
Evaluator	51
Excuses	29, 55
Exercise	18, 26
Exercise is cumulative	35
Exertion	44
Expectations	32

F

Failure	29
Farmer	65
Fat loss	35
Father	48
Fear	18, 50
Fear God	56
Fictitious danger	27
Finances	19, 31
Fire	54
Firecrackers	16
Fitness boot camp	38
Flexibility	42
Food	49
Foreigners	65
Forgiveness	10, 19, 60, 62
Form	43
Foul language	
toxic mental waste	24
Free time	35
Friend	18
Friendship	19
Frugality	23
Fulfillment	13

Full Metal Jacket 48
Future 30

G

Gasoline 35
Generosity 23
Gift 15, 60
Givers gain 13
Giving 10, 12, 15
    thanks 14
Goal setting 27, 31
Goals 26, 28
    long-term 27
    short-term 27
    state in present tense 29
God 16, 19, 23, 49, 54, 56
Golden Rule 8, 10, 49
Gossip 24
Government conspiracy 38
Gratitude 15, 16, 17, 57
Grudge 15, 60
Guidance 62

H

Happiness 19, 54, 56
Harvest 65
Hate 10, 48
Health 56
    wisdom 12
Health care costs 37
Health crisis 38
Health insurance 35, 39
Health pollution 34, 40
Heart 12, 19, 48, 50, 55

Heart disease	34
Help	50
High value tasks	31
Homeless	19, 56, 62
Honesty	14
Honor the Lord	64
Honorable	8, 16, 23
Hope	29, 62
Horses	54
How to look better	35
Humility	11, 14, 48, 49, 52, 53, 64
Hungry	49
Hurt	58

I

Illiterate	50
Impact	
more important than intentions	30
Inadequacy	13
Indifference	22, 63
Indifferent	17
Influence	17, 56
Insight	16
Instant gratification	39
Insult	60
Investment	26

J

James Bond	22
Jesus Christ	53, 56
Jog	44
Joy	19, 23

K

Kindness 10, 51, 62

L

Lactic acid 40
Land mines of life 29
Law of attraction 10, 51
Law of forgiving 51
Law of giving 10, 51
Law of Moses 48
Law of motion
    Isaac Newton 38
Leaders 39
Leader's attitude 40
Learning 15, 17
Legacy 11, 51
Lie 18
Life 22, 23
Life expectancy 38
Lifestyle 19, 34
Listen to the souls 59
Loneliness 13
Long-term goals 27, 29, 30
Long-term perspective 32
Longevity 41
    wisdom 12
Lord 48
Love 10, 48, 49, 54
Low-octane fuel 37

M

Marriage 11
Marriages 52
Master 52

Math	44
Meaning of seeking	57
Meaningless	24
Measure	55
Medical insurance	34
Medication	43
Medications	34, 40
Meditating	48
Mentality	22
Mercy	14
Military	18, 26, 31
Mind	15, 43
Mission	51
Mistakes	8, 30
Money	14, 15, 52
frugality	23
wise use	16
Motivation	26
Motive	9, 57
Multiplication	44
Muscle endurance	42
Muscle loss	35
Muscle mass	35
Muscle strength	42
Myths	
muscles	36
waist	36

N

Natural laws	12, 53
Needs	13
Needy	65
Negativity	14, 15, 17, 40
like a skunk	15
Networking	54

Never give up	32
Nonessentials	27
Nutritional food labels	43

O

Obesity	41
Oblivious	64
Old	18
Opportunities	21
Opportunity	52
Opposite of love	49
Outdoors	44
Overindulgence	39

P

Patience	23
Paycheck	65
Peace	21, 22, 64
Perhaps	57
permanent weight-loss obstacles	36
Perseverance	29
Personal development	11, 52
Perspective	12, 55
Pharmacy	34
Philosopher	53
Philosophies	53
Philosophy	18
Philosophy of movement	35
Philosophy of sedentary lifestyle	45
Pill popping mentality	45
Pills	22
Planning	26, 31
Playground	44

Point A to point B	26
Politics	18
Positive attitude	14
Positive change	30, 51
Positive emotions	14
Possibilities	20
Praise	10, 14, 51, 57, 63
debt	17
Pray	48
Prayer	14, 64
Praying	48
Predator	19
Predict the future	30
Prejudice	14
Prey	19
Priorities	19, 32
Productivity	37
Progress	21, 38, 44
Proverbs	9, 10, 12, 49, 50, 55, 64
Prudent person	9
Psyche	18
Purpose	11, 32, 52, 56
Push-ups	43

Q

Quality of life	16, 41, 52
Quantity of life	52
Questions	52
Quick-fixes	40

R

Race-car driver	37
Raisin theory	28
Reality	26, 29, 32

Refined foods 22, 40
Relationships 10, 24, 31, 50, 51, 54, 56
Religions 49, 53
Respect 8
Responsibility 9
Responsible
    health crisis 38
Right
    the right thing 15
Righteousness 60
Role models 39

S

Sabotage 8
Safe haven 54
Salvation 53
Savior 53
Schoolteachers
    high moral standards of conduct 39
Second chances 28
Secret 13
Secrets 56
Secular 49
Sedentary lifestyle 22, 39
Seeker 48, 64
Self-concept 21
Self-deception 34
Self-esteem 10, 16, 40, 51, 52
Self-evaluate 52
Self-talk 9
Self-worth 18, 22
Selfish 9
Selfishness 48
Sermon on the Mount 23, 64
Servants 13

Short-term goals	27
Silence	24
Slave	52
Slaves	13
Smile	12
Soul	15, 18, 48, 55, 56
Spirit	27
of God	19
Spirit of God	63
Spiritual	48
Standards	16
Status quo	54
Strategic planning	29, 32
Strength	62
Strength training	36
Stroke	34
Struggle	38
Substance	43
Success	54
Sun-Sentinel	57
Support	13, 21

T

Take charge of your life	30
Take nothing for granted	63
Task	30
high value	31
Teachable	15, 57
Teachers	39
Team building	38
Ten percent club	32
Test	51
Think	20, 21, 22
Thirsty	49
Thoughts	15, 23, 34, 55

Time... 11, 19, 26, 31, 42, 55
Toxic mental waste.. 22
Training... 51
Trash collector... 65
Treasure... 12, 55
Trends... 40
Troubled youth.. 63
True purpose.. 52, 54
Trust.. 56
Truth.. 10, 13, 16, 18, 48, 49, 50

U

Understanding... 22
Universal values.. 49

V

Values
    timeless.. 16
Victim.. 19
Victim mentality... 19
Visualization... 26, 42
Vulnerability... 49

W

Walk... 44
Walking meeting... 36
War... 11, 42
Warrior... 8
Weight loss... 26
Wellness
    corporate promotion.. 37
Wellness program... 38
Wisdom.................................... 11, 12, 16, 23, 50, 51, 54, 64

World 49, 52
Worth 12, 58

Y

Youth 19, 62

About the Author

Lt. Col. Bob Weinstein, USAR-Ret.

Born in Washington, D.C., Lt. Col. Bob Weinstein grew up in Virginia and spent 20 years in Berlin, Germany; he is retired from the United States Army Reserve as a Lieutenant Colonel with 30 years of service and spent about half that time as a senior military instructor with the Command & General Staff College.

He has been featured on radio and television, among others, on the History Channel and Fox Sports Net as well as in various publications such as the Washington Times, The Miami Herald and the Las Vegas Tribune.

His background is unique and diverse, including: military instructor, attorney, motivational speaker, wellness coach, certified corporate trainer, and certified personal trainer. He is fluent in German and English.

He is a popular motivational speaker at corporate events and banquets and conducts military-style workouts on Fort Lauderdale Beach utilizing strength, cardio, flexibility and agility training - both in personal training and group sessions.

He strongly believes in the importance of giving back to the community. Col. Weinstein volunteers his time for homeless and run-away kids at the Covenant House and also devotes time to training youth who are members of the US Naval Sea Cadets Corps, Team Spruance, Fort Lauderdale, Florida.

He is a member of the National Speakers Association and the American Council on Exercise.

He is the author of *Change Made Easy - Your Basic Training Orders to Excellent Physical and Mental Health.*, about personal development, fitness, exercise and health. Some of his previous clients as a guest speaker include: Sony, DHL, American Express, KPMG, AOL, IBM, AARP, SmithBarney, Green Bay Packers and Humana.

To purchase additional copies of this book or other
books or products by Lt. Col. Weinstein
call his toll free number at 1-888-768-9892

Or visit his website at:
www.TheHealthColonel.com

The Health Colonel Corporation
Fort Lauderdale, Florida, USA
"Changing the way people think about health."

Speaker Topics as Keynotes and Workshops by Lt. Col. Weinstein

The Eight Universal Laws of Getting and Staying in Shape

Over 3,000 Americans die of heart disease, cancer and stroke. Over eighty percent of these deaths are lifestyle related. Your organization will make sure that their employees do not become a lifestyle-related casualty of this war on fighting disease and maintaining good health.

Six Keys to Permanent Weight Loss

50 % of Americans are overweight, 33% are obese, and as many as 40% of women and 25% of men are trying to lose weight at any given time. We have a serious crisis of overeating and leading a sedentary lifestyle. This topic is designed to equip the audience with the necessary strategic and tactical knowledge to conquer these health issues.

Cost Effective Wellness Programs for Small, Medium and Large Businesses

According to the Centers for Disease Control, more than 75% of employer health care costs and productivity losses are related to employee lifestyle choices. Other studies have revealed that about 20% are responsible for 80% of the costs. You will be given the necessary tools to immediately implement a cost effective wellness program that significantly improves the health and performance of your employees.

How to Combat Childhood Obesity

The percentage of our youth who are overweight has tripled since the early 1970's. Col. Weinstein addresses the six "secrets" to combating the youth health crisis. We are killing our children and preparing them to have serious health issues early in life. You will be pointed in the right direction to guide and inspire our youth to lead healthy and happy lives.

Give-up vs. Take-charge Talk

Getting back on track with performance based living is a matter of how we think. You will learn how to identify and eliminate what Col. Weinstein calls give-up talk and replace it with take-charge talk when it comes to healthy living.

Call 954-636-5351 to book Col. Weinstein as a speaker.

Speaker Topics as Keynotes and Workshops by Lt. Col. Weinstein

Get Back Up and Catch Your Second Wind!

We've all heard the expression "Catch your second wind!" Unfortunately, the vast majority of people don't even know what the second wind feels like and there is a reason for this. Ninety percent usually give-up as soon as the first difficulties or challenges occur. Col. Weinstein will give you those insights necessary to take you and your worthy goals into the realm of the second wind and keep up that momentum.

Values and Character Matter Most

There is no exception. Values and character do matter most and are foundational for sound relationships in the business world and in our family lives. Whether you are interested in furthering your career, building high performance teams or showing our youth or adults the way to lead a truly values-based life, this is the topic for you and your organization.

Six Keys to Weight Management

We have serious health issues related to unhealthy lifestyles and over-eating. Medical costs are souring and lives are lost. Fit and healthy Americans translates into less illness, more work productivity, more energy and happier Americans. Col. Weinstein maps out a strategy to keep the weight under control and have more energy. This topic is not just for those wanting to lose weight. The same strategies apply to healthy weight management.

Team Building

Working together is a huge productivity booster. Col. Weinstein will help build your team with a variety of activities and adding a dose of humor, entertainment and fun. Recommended for all types of businesses.

Call 954-636-5351 to book Col. Weinstein as a speaker.

More Products from the Health Colonel
Use quick order form on next page or go to
www.TheHealthColonel.com for EASY ONLINE ORDERING.

Get Your Priorities Straight

Put an end to indecisiveness and take back control of your life. Learn to move out with confidence and purpose. Learn to overcome life obstacles. Discover your true life priorities and how to implement them. Find out how to reinvent your life into the true you that is already inside and waiting to be allowed to live life to the fullest. Discover the ultimate law of happiness and learn how to apply it today.
Audio CD: $11.95 (30 min.)

Quotes to Live By

My personal journey to seek out wisdom and improvement in my life and the lives of others has resulted in this collection of quotes. May they inspire you or someone you know to be a better person and always take the high road when faced with challenging decisions. The journey is still in progress for me and will last a lifetime.
Paperback: $7.99 (72 pages)

Six Keys to Permanent Weight-loss

Join the Fitness and Beach Boot Camp Instructor, Lt. Col. Bob Weinstein, USAR, (ret.), on his over 60 minute journey to successful and permanent weight loss, delivered with enthusiasm, humor and high energy. You will tap into the vast experience of the Health Colonel. You will talk, think and eat yourself lean after following Colonel Weinstein's straightforward, no-nonsense, Six Keys to Permanent Weight Loss.
Audio CD: $11.99 (60 min.)

More Products from the Health Colonel
Use quick order form on next page or go to
www.TheHealthColonel.com for EASY ONLINE ORDERING.

Change Made Easy - Your Basic Training Orders to Excellent Physical and Mental Health

Put on your commander's hat. You are about to take charge of your health. This book is a health and fitness blueprint to get America back in shape, keep Americans from dying of ill health and keep Americans strong. A combination of self-help, right eating, exercising, how to start a fitness boot camp, weight loss as well as guidance on how to lead a values-based life to the benefit of others and our society. Lots of exercise photos.
Paperback: $14.99 (256 pages)

Eight Secrets to Longevity, Health and Fitness

An exciting journey to empower and educate you to take charge of your health and eating habits. Put on your commander's hat and take charge of your all those body parts that may not be firm as they used to. Delivered with enthusiasm, humor and high energy. You will tap into the vast experience of the Health Colonel. A Straight-forward, no-nonsense, back-to-basics approach to exercise and eating.
Audio CD: $11.99 (54 min.)

Beach Boot Camp Upper Body Blast

Suitable for all fitness levels and excellent for group exercise instruction. This video is much more than those follow-along workout routines on the market. It includes great workout tips, humor, great beach scenes and inspirational and motivational guidance all wrapped into this dynamic 29 minute program. The workout is filmed on Fort Lauderdale Beach in Florida. Join him with his group class as he equips and empowers you to take your workout to the next level. Both natural body weight exercises as well as some using an inexpensive rubber resistance band are demonstrated.
DVD Video: $14.95 (29 min.)

More Products from the Health Colonel
Use quick order form on next page or go to
www.TheHealthColonel.com for EASY ONLINE ORDERING

Weight Loss - Twenty Pounds in Ten Weeks - Move It to Lose It

Weight Loss and weight management book with a ten week exercise and eating plan to lose twenty pounds. Full of easy-to-use tools to organize and implement the program: exercise photos, ten week exercise chart, 1,200 and 1,600 calorie menus, calorie burn charts, workout log, food diary and more. The author, Lt. Col. Weinstein has been featured on the History Channel. Paperback: $18.00 (218 pages)

THEHEALTHCOLONEL.COM

Changing the way people think about health.

QUICK ORDER FORM

Fax orders: 866-481-2804. Send this form.

Telephone orders: Call 888-768-9892 toll-free

Email orders: thehealthcolonel@beachbootcamp.net

Postal orders: The Health Colonel, Lt. Col. Bob Weinstein, USAR-Ret., 757 SE 17th Street, #267, Fort Lauderdale, FL 33316, Telephone 954-636-5351

Please send the following books, audio CDs, DVDs:

_____
_____
_____

Please send more FREE information on:

❑ Other books   ❑ Speaking/seminars

❑ Fitness Boot Camp ❑ Mailing Lists

Name:_____

Address:_____

City:_____State:_____Zip:_____

Telephone:_____

Email address:_____

Sales tax: Please add Florida sales tax for products shipped to Florida addresses.

Shipping:
U.S.: $4.50 for first book, CD or DVD and $2.50 for each additional product.
International: $9.50 for first product; $5.50 for each additional product (estimate).

THEHEALTHCOLONEL.COM

CHANGING THE WAY PEOPLE THINK ABOUT HEALTH.

QUICK ORDER FORM

Fax orders: 866-481-2804. Send this form.

Telephone orders: Call 888-768-9892 toll-free

Email orders: thehealthcolonel@beachbootcamp.net

Postal orders: The Health Colonel, Lt. Col. Bob Weinstein, USAR-Ret., 757 SE 17th Street, #267, Fort Lauderdale, FL 33316, Telephone 954-636-5351

Please send the following books, audio CDs, DVDs:

_____
_____
_____

Please send more FREE information on:

❏ Other books ❏ Speaking/seminars

❏ Fitness Boot Camp ❏ Mailing Lists

Name:_____

Address:_____

City:_____State:_____Zip:_____

Telephone:_____

Email address:_____

Sales tax: Please add Florida sales tax for products shipped to Florida addresses.

Shipping:
U.S.: $4.50 for first book, CD or DVD and $2.50 for each additional product.
International: $9.50 for first product; $5.50 for each additional product (estimate).

THEHEALTHCOLONEL.COM

CHANGING THE WAY PEOPLE THINK ABOUT HEALTH.

QUICK ORDER FORM

Fax orders: 866-481-2804. Send this form.

Telephone orders: Call 888-768-9892 toll-free

Email orders: thehealthcolonel@beachbootcamp.net

Postal orders: The Health Colonel, Lt. Col. Bob Weinstein, USAR-Ret., 757 SE 17th Street, #267, Fort Lauderdale, FL 33316, Telephone 954-636-5351

Please send the following books, audio CDs, DVDs:

_____
_____
_____

Please send more FREE information on:

❏ Other books ❏ Speaking/seminars

❏ Fitness Boot Camp ❏ Mailing Lists

Name:_____

Address:_____

City:_____State:_____Zip:_____

Telephone:_____

Email address:_____

Sales tax: Please add Florida sales tax for products shipped to Florida addresses.

Shipping:
U.S.: $4.50 for first book, CD or DVD and $2.50 for each additional product.
International: $9.50 for first product; $5.50 for each additional product (estimate).

www.ingramcontent.com/pod-product-compliance
Lightning Source LLC
Chambersburg PA
CBHW020015050426
42450CB00005B/485